Bahna Pyramid of Selling Effectiveness

People Buy on Emotion and Justify it Logically.

People Buy for What they IMAGINE Something will do for them.

- Exceed Expectations
- Confidence and Momentum
- Build Trust and Credibility
- Competitiveness/Competition
- Story Selling/Creativity
- High-Gain Questions
- Couching and Timing of Questions
- WIIFMs/So What?
- Steps of the Sales Call
- Mutual Accountability/Shorten the Sales Cycle
- Product/Clinical Knowledge
- What Does Good Look Like?/Do the Right Things Every Day
- Attitude and Work Ethic

12 Lessons In Selling

1. Set Daily Goals - 5 extra/day
2. Become a Student of Selling
3. Always Bring Value
4. You Can Help Them if They Let You
5. Follow the 80/20 Rule
6. Reasons vs Excuse
7. Prepare to Win - Pre-call Planning
8. Gain Customer Commitment
9. Never Present Until You Uncover a Need
10. Outwork Everyone Else
11. Plant the Next Steps
12. Invest in Yourself

Level 8: High-Gain Questions

"Your past is important because it brought you to where you are, but as important as your past is, it is not nearly as important as the way you see your future." **Dr. Tony Campolo**

As people trying to *influence behaviors and results,* it is critical that we stay one or two steps ahead of industry trends to avoid getting the same objections and negative responses from people who learn *"response behaviors"* based on what other people do, say, and ask. This is important in all aspects of learning, training, coaching, and influencing behavior of any kind.

We *learn behaviors* from our experiences. When we are trying to influence others, we need to take into account the *behaviors they learned* as a result of their experiences. A new dad may be nervous changing a diaper, but when the third child comes around his comfort zone is completely different, and he can change the kid upside down while not missing the big play in the game if necessary.

I would like to believe that my wife Jenny and I are pretty generous people as it relates to charitable giving. Beyond normal taxes and the causes we support through our government, we donate money, materials, time, and support great charities of our choosing. Most of those charities work with animals and children because we feel they are often the least able to influence positive outcomes on their own. (Jenny worked as a social worker for 15+ years).

It is difficult to go into a gas station, convenience store or just about anywhere you spend money today and not be asked if you want to donate money to one charity or another when you check out. Clearly, this gets more donations than not asking for that particular charity.

However, since there are multiple gas stations to choose from in most locations, it may turn off customers and influence them in ways that the proprietor did not intend. This is especially true if I happen to know that the charity has a poor track record, or I do not believe in the cause since they pay their CEO $750,000 per year with unlimited access to a private jet.

After you are asked multiple times at different places - you may become *conditioned to say "no"* without even thinking about it or hearing the message. I may not even know which charity I am being asked about before mumbling *"no thanks"* to the poor clerk who does not even want to ask, but is doing their job.

While I was growing up, McDonald's was one of the first restaurants I remember asking if you wanted to add another item with your order – *"upselling."* I remember when they started asking if you wanted to add a *hot apple pie* to your order. I am sure that worked for a while, and *apple pie* sales rose to a certain level and then evened out. Then they switched to *cookies, sundaes* and eventually to *fries, biggie sizing, value meals* and *dollar menus*. Why? Because customers *learned responses* and they saw the success rates evening out. When other restaurants started *"upselling,"* results were further impacted.

How often have you thought *"If I wanted fries with my order, I would have asked."* I would venture to guess that for most of us, that *learned response* happened after we had been asked numerous times. In the beginning, it was new and a different approach.

When you are trying to influence behaviors, remember the impact of comfort zones and prior experiences. *If you do the same thing everyone else does, you will get similar results.* Ask better questions that make them stop, think and share – not the same questions everyone else asks that elicit *rote, learned answers*. We need to *differentiate* ourselves and our companies.

If Jenny and I owned, or managed a full-service restaurant, we would incorporate two rules for our teams. *First*, one person would have the sole responsibility of making sure people's drink glasses were filled. Water, soda, juices and most importantly for profit – wine, beer, and other spirits. No one should ever wait for those items, and if you had a specialist walking around dedicated to that task, you would get positive responses. How often would you have ordered one more drink, but by the time they asked the meal was almost finished?

Revenue, expenses, and profit margins would be topics we regularly talked about with our team hoping everyone felt responsibility, and we were *rowing in the same direction*.

The Second rule involves desserts. We would not ask *"do you want to see a dessert menu?"* We know we should not add the extra calories! We would bring out the desert tray and let them see the carrot cake, cheesecake, chocolate cake, key lime pie and Crème Brule and sell them on how good they are when they were right in front of them. If they said *"no,"* at a minimum we would ask *"which one they would like to share for the table."*

Effective Communication

Do you know someone who makes people feel like they are the only person in the room, or the most important person in the world during a conversation? Chances are they were *effective communicators*, including being active listeners, and ask good *open-ended questions*. They probably have you talking much more than they talk in a *one-on-one situation*.

Effective communication is the process of exchanging ideas, thoughts, opinions, knowledge, and data so that the message is **received** and **understood** with clarity and purpose. It involves being *clear, correct, complete, concise*, and *compassionate* in conveying a message. We often talk about *effective communication* in terms of speech, but it should occur in various forms: verbal and non-verbal, written, visual, and with listening skills. It is essential for *building trust, resolving conflicts, and fostering strong relationships in both personal and professional settings.*

Effective communication is about more than just exchanging information; it involves understanding the emotions and intentions behind the information and ensuring that the message is received and understood **as intended**.

Pausing is an important communication skill that salespeople should embrace and utilize. Work to achieve a comfort level with *pausing* to give you time to think, and allow the customer to interject as much as possible.

Effective Communication requires an understanding of *intent* and that requires *context*. While email and texting are quick and convenient, it is easy to lose control of the *intent* and *context*. There is no substitute for *live communication*, and as a salesperson you can *control live situations* and *recreate emotions*.

Have you received an email or text and fired off a quick response because the message made you mad? Are you sure that is what the sender intended? What if spellcheck automatically changed their message? What if they were driving? What if they were in a hurry?

If an email or text frustrates you, wait long enough before responding so it is no longer an emotional response on your part.

Asking the right questions is a skill that significantly contributes to effective communication, fostering understanding, alignment, and preventing miscommunication.

Like any skill, you can improve your questions, follow-up questions and ultimately your results by working at it and becoming better. Be a student of communication – it is all around you. *What commercials work? What ads caught your eye? What questions do others ask you that make you open up and share? What questions do you ask that don't get you where you want to go?*

Active listening is an important skill in effective communication. *Active listening* involves fully concentrating, understanding, responding, and remembering what is being said. It is a way of listening and responding to another person that improves mutual understanding. You may have heard it said that *active listening* is listening so that *you understand what it being said*, versus *listening to respond*.

By *actively listening*, a sense of belonging and mutual understanding is created between individuals. It is an important skill for leaders, as it will inspire respect and lead to improvements in professional and personal relationships.

Paraphrasing, taking notes, repeating their words back to them, and asking more in-depth follow-up questions show you are *actively listening*. Even during a phone conversation, I let the other person know I am taking notes, so I send the message that what they say is important to me. Feeling like the other person listened, understands our situation, and cares makes a big impact in our *level of trust*.

- *Have I said anything that's raised any concerns?*
- *Before we move on, the floor is yours – any questions nagging at you that you'd like me to answer?*

Hearing is listening to what is said. **Listening** is hearing what is not said.

Barbara Walters Interview/Question Techniques

For years *Barbara Walters* was known for her effective interview techniques, which involved extensive preparation and the ability to ask tough and thought-provoking questions. She thoroughly prepared (or her staff did) for interviews and emphasized the importance of extensive research and understanding her subjects.

Walters stated, "*Well, the first thing I tell anybody who's going to be doing interviews is do your homework. I do *so much homework, I know more about the person than he or she does about himself"*

She would write down lists of fifty or a hundred questions on little cards, put them in order, and then spend hours or days changing the order of the questions. *Walters* believed in knowing her questions so well that she could throw all the cards away if necessary.

Walters would often ask about her interviewees' childhood and their relationship with their parents to elicit *emotional responses*. This thorough preparation and strategic question planning were key elements of her interviewing style.

Her approach to follow-up questions during interviews involved being genuinely curious and using carefully choreographed questions to elicit unexpected responses. Walters believed in asking questions that would make the interviewee *think* and *tell her something she hadn't heard before.*

Often, the subjects of her interviews would say, *"Barbara, I have never shared this before,"* or *"I have not said this publicly before."*

This approach allowed her to delve deeper into the subject matter and elicit more insightful and revealing responses from her interviewees. It worked to keep everyone engaged – including the interviewee and the audience.

Barbara Walter's key strategies mirror that of what a good salesperson does, and included:

- *Extensive Research:* Walters emphasized the importance of thorough research before an interview, often knowing more about the interviewee than they knew about themselves.
- *Asking Provocative Questions*: She was known for asking questions that made people think and revealed new information, such as inquiring about a person's philosophy or asking about the biggest misconception about them.
- *Tough Questioning:* Walters was not afraid to ask tough questions, often saving the most difficult ones for the end of the interview.
- *Creating a Story with Questions and Answers:* She organized her questions around subjects and themes, creating a narrative with her questions and the interviewee's answers.

High-Gain Questions

High-gain questions are *thought-provoking questions that seek to gain the most valuable information from a prospect, as efficiently as possible.* The goal is to ask a question that makes them *stop and think prior to answering.* These types of questions are the *secret sauce* to any good interview or conversation that draws out information.

How many questions are our customer asked each week by salespeople? If they engage with *5 salespeople each day*, and the salesperson ask them *3 questions*, that is *15 questions per day*, **75 in a week**. If you finish the math it comes out to around *3600* questions per year. No wonder they *learn responses* and get bored! We need to *differentiate our questions* to help us get *better information* and *set us apart*.

A great number of the questions salespeople traditionally ask only elicit *rote (reflexive and automatic)* answers. We need the answers to those questions, but the more research and preparation we do, the more time we save for better, thought-provoking questions with key decision makers. Take the most basic *fact-finding questions* and ask other people in the organization for that information if you cannot find it in your research.

"Janet, I have a few fact-finding questions for information that was not readily available during my research and discussions so far. So you and I maximize our time when we meet in 2 weeks, and I am best prepared to discuss which solutions might make the most sense for your department, who would you direct me to in your area to get some of that information?"

As you probably experienced if you used an approach like this, they often come back and ask, *"What type of information?"* You may find the conversation picks up steam again and goes on immediately.

High-gain questions are useful in gathering deeper information faster, improving the quality of your conversations, and increasing the chances of closing deals more efficiently.

When salespeople enter conversations with prospects, we do so with the same basic objectives:

1. Learn as much as they can about the prospect and their pain points.
2. Tailor our presentation to help them see why our product or solution is exactly what they need.
3. Put the prospect on a path toward mutual success.

If salespeople go after the same objectives, why do some succeed while others fail? Ultimately, success during sales conversations is strongly impacted by the **questions** they ask and how they ask for it.

High-gain questions should be thought-provoking questions that get the prospect to think deeply about their business, pain points, purchasing decisions, and potential solutions.

- "John, I understand you are discussing (X) as a potential new protocol for (Y). What are your thoughts on how that change would impact your department, and what do you see as the potential benefits?"

- "Janet, I read two articles recently that seemed to come to the opposite conclusions about (issue). One group of authors suggested (X), while the other group suggested (Y). I am curious to hear what your opinion is on (issue)?"
- "Jenny, I love to ask this next question because (title) generally answer it in the same way, but sometimes I get surprised. What is your opinion about (issue)?"
- "In working with other (title) all over the state, they have shared their priorities for 20.. and what they are trying to achieve in terms of improvements in (department or issue). What are your top 3 priorities for 20..?"

One benefit of high-gain questions is that they allow you to mention *sensitive information* and not give away your *opinion or position* up front. This helps soften the discussion of controversial topics, and allow them to feel in control, while you are actually directing the conversation.

- "I understand you have been a Nurse Manager for 10 years. What are the biggest changes you have seen in that time as it relates to how your responsibilities evolved? Where do you find yourself spending a lot of time where you didn't use to?"

- "(Company) has unique clinical solutions to help with (issue) – which seems to be an area more of our customers are re-evaluating. Could you please share with me your current process or protocols that are in place for (procedure)."
- "We specialize in working with hospitals in my territory (which is....). I am surprised by the variety of answers I get when I ask this question. What are the top priorities you have in terms of projects or performance improvement as you head into 20..?"
- "A recent study in the (date and publication name) indicated that (fact or conclusion from article)."
    - "Could you please share with me how this compares to your experience in this area?"
    - "What are your thoughts on those conclusions?"

Write out 2 high-gain questions to use on 2 scheduled sales calls.

40 other questions to steer the conversation in the right direction:

- What led you to take this call today?

- *What are your most important priorities in your role at your company?*
- *What is the biggest obstacle that has stopped or hindered you from fulfilling these priorities?*
- *How long have you been dealing with this issue?*
- *What are the day-to-day consequences this (issue) has caused? Can you give me examples of what you've had to deal with?*
- *Who else is impacted by this (issue)?*
- *Outside of its impact on the business, how much of an impact has this problem had on you personally? What has bothered you the most about this issue?*
- *What other challenges are you experiencing? Are these secondary issues a result of your main problem or separate issues?*
- *We just discussed [X pain point]. How urgently do you need to solve this problem?*
- *When do you hope to have a solution in place?*
- *When making purchases of this size and scope in the past, how long did the deal take to finalize?*
- *Barring any roadblocks, how long do you anticipate it'll take to make a decision on this deal?*

- What would we need to do to ensure we meet a timeline of [X]?
- In order to start [specific project] we'll need [specific deliverables]. What do you need from me to make sure you're able to hit those deadlines and keep this initiative on track?
- How have you attempted to solve this issue in the past?
- Which other products and services have you tried or considered trying?
- What would a product or solution need to offer to win your business?
- What criteria are you using to evaluate [specific type of product]?
- How does my product stack up to the others you're evaluating?
- Based on what we've discussed, can you think of any potential roadblocks that might come up?
- Knowing the other stakeholders, do you foresee any objections or concerns they might have about this solution?
- When you've been a part of similar deals in the past, did you run into any problems that we can hopefully avoid here?
- Imagine the worst-case scenario for me: what's the one thing that would have to happen in order for the deal to fall apart?
- When we first talked, your main priority was [specific initiative], is that still the case?

- You were originally hoping to launch [specific initiative] by [specific date], is this still a main priority for you?
- Is there any documentation you need from me to make internal discussions about my product easier?
- Have I done a good job showing you how [specific product] solves [specific problem]? Or is there something else you'd like to see or discuss?
- What do you see as the biggest factor or influence on your decision to buy?
- What budget do you have allocated for this solution?
- How does your company typically budget for solutions like this?
- Has budget been an issue when you've looked at solving these problems in the past?
- A customer who is comparable to your company spends somewhere around [X] per month on [X solution]. Does that align with what you're looking to spend?
- We estimate that a company like yours could gain [X] per quarter by solving the problems you've told me about. What does your budget look like in comparison?
- How flexible is the budget range you've provided?

- What requirements would a tool or service need to meet in order for your company to spend money on it?
- How did your team decide on your budget for this project?
- What would the financial impact be on your company if you were to continue doing [task] the way you're doing it now?
- How much money would solving [specific problem] save your company?
- I know you're incredibly busy. In order to make sure we're aligned on pricing and budget, and to save us both the time, when do you think it makes sense to discuss pricing?
- Is there anything I can do to help you understand or justify spending money on our product?

Pick 5 questions and commit to using them in the next week. Track your results.

Trial Lawyers

I am intrigued by the similarities in *skills and strategies* that both good *trial lawyers* and good *salespeople* utilize in their craft. The best look several steps ahead, anticipating what the answers will be and preparing to control the dialogue.

During witness testimony (questioning) they try not to ask questions that they *do not already know the answer to* so that they are not caught off guard. They can lose a trial, like we might lose a sale, if an answer in front of the jury (group) is one that causes enough doubt.

Compelling Opening: Trial lawyers and their teams spend a significant amount of time preparing a compelling *opening statement*. Research shows that most jurors arrive at their verdict during or immediately after opening statements (so much for *evidence* and being *innocent until proven guilty*). I believe that good openings make or break how effective salespeople are on their calls. If the customer does not agree to move forward in the discussion, you are pretty much *"dead in the water."*

I had to look it up, so here you go for those that did not know: *"dead in the water"* originated as a *nautical term*, referring to a motionless sail ship on a windless day, which appeared to be without momentum or any chance of progression.

Understanding the Audience: Trial lawyers research jurors' backgrounds, experience, and beliefs to both pick a jury, and develop a winning strategy. Unfortunately, as much as we would like to sometimes, salespeople usually do not get the chance to *disqualify people from the buying process*. Having a good understanding of the buyers' needs, experience, and goals before a presentation or meeting will help us present our case effectively.

Always "On Stage": In both the courtroom and sales, professionals are constantly being observed. In sales, how you handle questions, and how you treat everyone who contributes to the overall impression you make.

Closing on Emotions: Trial lawyers use their closing statement to make one last appeal to jurors' emotions, as research shows that emotions play a major role in decision making. We know how important emotion and closing are in sales.

Be Up Front About Your Weaknesses: Honesty and transparency are important in both legal arguments and sales. Being upfront about weaknesses will help build trust with clients, and prevent objections or doubts from being their focus when they go to deliberation/committee meetings.

The *most effective salespeople* ask the *most effective questions*. Make sure the ones you use provide the information you need, are not yes/no, or providing one-word answers if you are trying to open up dialogue and uncover needs and challenges. Become an expert at asking great questions and you will see your positive results increase.

Pay special attention to your follow-up questions. When someone gives you a crack, you need to **kick in**

the door. Salespeople often stop one or two questions too early. Quantify it, bring out more emotion and pain.

"How would that impact (X)":

"What would the long-term effects be on":

- Cost
- Staff Impact
- Patient Reactions
- Board
- Boss
- Your day/week
- Achievement of your goals

High-gain questions will differentiate you. Ask 2 top salespeople for examples of what they use effectively.

Understand the Purchasing Process and Professional Buyers

Procurement, purchasing, materials management, buyer, sourcing agent, category manager, whatever the title, many of these professionals do a fantastic job for their organizations. As a sales professional it is important to understand the world of everyone we are engaged with in the sales process.

Purchasing professionals use their procurement skills, negotiation abilities, cost-saving strategies, and vendor relationships to ensure timely delivery of goods, maintain inventory levels, adhere to internal and external regulations and policies, manage internal systems and programs.

Depending on the size and complexity of the organization, manufacturing needs and capabilities, group purchasing contracts, committee involvement, reporting requirements, and budget responsibilities, they may be involved and evaluated on other areas as well.

In some organizations, they also can be involved in the **"gatekeeper"** process to help manage access to employees and staff for a variety of reasons. They serve very important functions in organizations. And they deal with salespeople all day long.

Unfortunately, many salespeople look at **purchasing** as an **adversary** and do not put in the time or do a good job developing relationships with people in this area. That can lead to delays, unnecessary discounts, shopping opportunities, and lost sales. Professional salespeople should operate as if their competitors have a good relationship with the people in purchasing, and act accordingly.

The **purchasing cycle** within an organization encompasses their entire process of processing a purchase order from initiation to completion. What is important for **salespeople** to understand is that **their best position of strength** is to be involved as **early in**

the process as possible. If you are the one helping them **identify the need,** you likely stand the best chance of ultimately winning the sale.

The **Purchasing-Procurement Center** identifies 11 Steps in the Standard Procurement Cycle, and adds a few more if a **Request for Proposal (RFP)** and **Bid/Tender** process is involved.

1) The Need
2) Specify – how many or how much
3) Requisition or order
4) Financial Authority
5) Research Suppliers
6) Choose Supplier
7) Establish Price and Terms
8) Place Order
9) Order Received and Inspected
10) Approval and Payment
11) Update of Records

If you are involved in the beginning, and the one helping them **uncover the need,** you can be at a distinct advantage. In some cases, if it does need to go through the **RFP process,** you may be able to be involved in writing the **specifications** for the bid, including putting features or benefits that make your product or service the likely winner.

Generally speaking, **salespeople** are paid more for their ability to influence the purchasing process earlier in the cycle. **Inbound orders**, where customers are calling a company to order, often due to marketing or advertisements, are usually later in the sales cycle and the representatives handling those are not going to be paid at the same level as those creating sales.

One additional challenge in today's market is the availability of and access to information for research and negotiations by a **professional purchasing person**. They often come in more prepared than the salesperson. We had a meeting with a professional purchasing agent who had clearly read our public annual report prior to the meeting, and referenced our **profit margins** and **EBITDA** compared to peers in the market during the **price negotiations**.

Depending on **what you sell, where you come in during the purchasing cycle**, the **purchasing people** you are working with, and the **industry**, you are likely to hear many of the following at some point:

- *Sharpen your pencil*
- *We looked at average pricing/benchmarking*
- *I can get it from x for y*
- *Your competitor sells it for*
- *Last time we paid*
- *Is it on contract?*
- *Are you a part of this buying group?*
- *Quantity discount. How much if I buy 50? Great, I want that price but only 20.*
- *Why can I get it for less from?*

- Will you be running any discounts/end of year specials?
- We are required to get 2/3 quotes. Who else sells it?
- I need a cost analysis showing
- When I get pushback on cost, how do I win? I need to show some reduction
- There is a new competitor
- Your annual report shows an EBITDA of x, 5 points higher than industry average. You can shave off a few points
- This will now come out of my budget, it did not before
- That is a fixed/soft cost that is not really a savings
- Is there a reimbursement code for this?
- Are others charging patients/customers for this?
- Why are you so expensive?
- Why has you price increased by xx%
- What is the cost per use? Including service/maintenance?
- What is the total cost of ownership?

If you are a **sales leader**, your job should include helping your team handle these **professionally** and **confidently** without hurting the relationship. These are not necessarily **objections**; they can be part of the **negotiation process.** Understanding the difference, depending on **when** and **how** they happen in the

purchasing cycle, and your **position of strength** are keys to a win-win outcome.

Practice your responses to these questions. The best replies often involve giving person **options** – so they feel like they are in **control,** and they have something to take back to **their boss** showing what they were able to **accomplish**.

"We understand the price increase impacts budgets. As you have seen, other suppliers are also being forced to increase prices due to inflation, interest rates, higher material, and shipping costs..

What we can do is look at this as a 3-year agreement. At the end of the agreement, we need the average price to be $100. To help with your budgeting, we can do $90 this year, $100 next year, and $110 the following year to get us to the $100 average. Or we can go to $100 now. Which would you prefer?"

That does not mean they are going to be thrilled with the price increase, but when you give **options** it can help them feel better about having some control, and give them something to **show as a win** during their **internal discussions**.

Bahna Pyramid of Selling Effectiveness

People Buy on Emotion and Justify it Logically.

People Buy for What they IMAGINE Something will do for them.

- Exceed Expectations
- Confidence and Momentum
- Build Trust and Credibility
- Competitiveness/Competition
- Story Selling/Creativity
- High-Gain Questions
- Couching and Timing of Questions
- WIIFMs/So What?
- Steps of the Sales Call
- Mutual Accountability/Shorten the Sales Cycle
- Product/Clinical Knowledge
- What Does Good Look Like?/Do the Right Things Every Day
- Attitude and Work Ethic

12 Lessons In Selling

1. Set Daily Goals - 5 extra/day
2. Become a Student of Selling
3. Always Bring Value
4. You Can Help Them if They Let You
5. Follow the 80/20 Rule
6. Reasons vs Excuse
7. Prepare to Win - Pre-call Planning
8. Gain Customer Commitment
9. Never Present Until You Uncover a Need
10. Outwork Everyone Else
11. Plant the Next Steps
12. Invest in Yourself

End Notes

Barbara Walters: The Art of the Interview. ABC News. Abcnews.go.com. May 16, 2014.

www.ingramcontent.com/pod-product-compliance
Lightning Source LLC
Chambersburg PA
CBHW071000220526
45471CB00007B/3115